THE OFFICIAL
ROCK PAPER SCISSORS
STRATEGY GUIDE

This book is a part of the
World Rock Paper Scissors Association
Library of Books.

For more information about the
World Rock Paper Scissors Association please visit
www.wrpsa.com

TABLE OF CONTENTS

INTRODUCTION

You might think, do we really need a Rock Paper Scissors Handbook? Yes! Rock Paper Scissors is the greatest hand game in the world. It is the most commonly played and easiest to learn. It can be used to settle a debate, or just for fun. There is no language needed and no setup required. A game that some may think is similar to a coin flip, in this book you will learn it is far more than that.

This book is intended to provide you with all the information you will ever need about the great sport of Rock Paper Scissors. In doing this our goal is that you will be able to realize your full potential. Learn the Rules, Strategies, Gambit Play, and Game Theory, and how it all contributes to the enjoyment of Rock Paper Scissors...along with Psychology, Etiquette, and all the Jokes we could think of and find for this incredible sport.

The World Rock Paper Scissors Association (WRPSA) was created to bring honesty and integrity back to the most played hand game in the world and intended to provide a foundation for the hand sport which no organization has done in the past. We are the preferred destination for anyone interested in the sport of Rock Paper Scissors. We have spent years playing and researching this sport. Everything we have learned about Rock Paper Scissors is included in this Handbook.

BASIC RULES OF ROCK PAPER SCISSORS

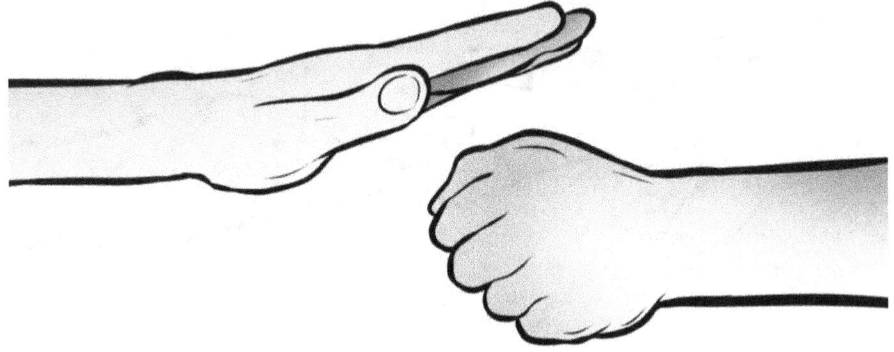

Paper Covers Rock

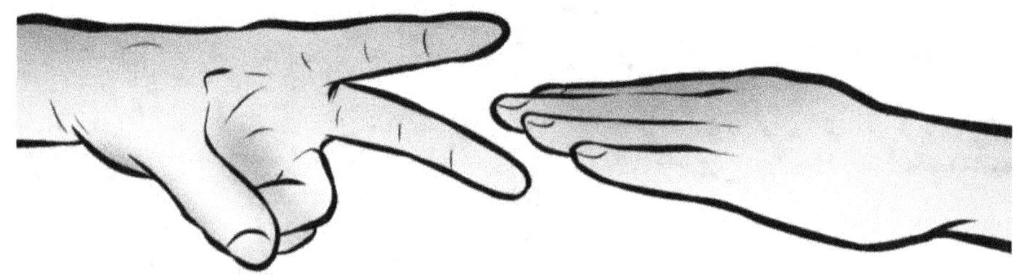

Scissors Cuts Paper

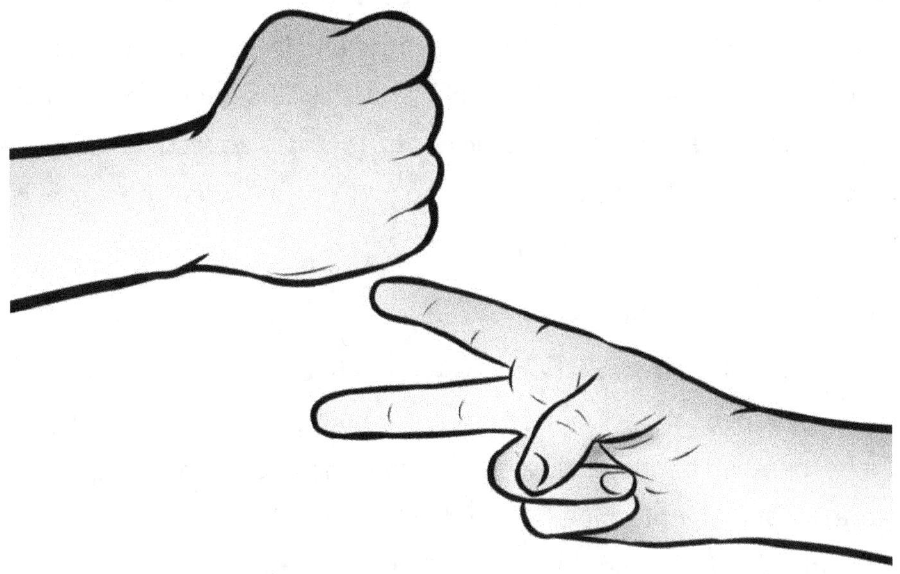

Rock Smashes Scissors

Rock Paper Scissors is an interesting game, there is no doubt about that. Although for some people who cannot handle the pressures, fearful anticipation, or the tense atmosphere, there may be some reservations. Generally, however, the Rock Paper Scissors game is one hell of a game. The positive reviews of people concerning the game beat the criticisms the game has met with since its development. As a result of the interest that many people continue to show the game, its popularity and influence continue to increase across the globe. The Rock Paper Scissors game is not only bringing in more interested participants. It is also attracting the curiosity of viewers or spectators who want to see what the game is about and how it is being played.

One of the reservations you would hear from people against the Rock Paper Scissors game is that it is evil. Their reasons for this are best known to them. However, studies have proven that the game is not evil, not made by the devil, nor made for those who dine with the devil. The Rock Paper Scissors game is pure and continues to be celebrated as a game for gentlemen. The game is for everyone and can be played in any part of the world as long as the participants exhibit some level of professionalism and respect for the game. To tell you how popular and fun the game has become, kids now play it among themselves in the streets, parks, schools, and social gatherings. In some cases, even, it has been discovered that the Rock Paper Scissors game is used to settle matters among brothers like who should wash the dishes or trim the garden.

In essence, the Rock Paper Scissors game has become a household thing as much as it is a formal and regulated engagement between professional participants. People enjoy it and will, at every chance they get, try their psychology in winning. Of course, who would not want to master a few hand gestures to compete with another person? Think about the training, mindfulness, mastery, and artistic creation involved in the process of throwing moves to win against your opponent. The game can even be considered as a technique to train your mind to be super conscious while trying to read the mind of your opponent. The Rock Paper Scissors game is not just a game and not a common one for that matter. The game is of the mind, requires movement and mastery of the game. Perhaps this is the reason why some consider the game evil, considering the psychology involved.

One of the things that should be noted about the Rock Paper Scissors game is that it is not alien, whether in nature or its application. It is human-made and therefore has its own unique history and origin. It is correct to say that every other game you can find around has their origins too. This simply means that something must have made up the idea for the game. Essentially, every game, whether online, offline, or physical, has its own purpose. Therefore, whatever makes up the purpose of a game is what the game will be played towards.

To put it in another way, there is a cause or reason for every game. For instance, the purpose of a soccer game is to kick the ball inside either of the nets. In the same way, there is a reason for the Rock Paper Scissors game.

The purpose of the Rock Paper Scissors game is to create a scene where the participants throw a series of moves in order to crush each other. The participants are usually two, and hand gestures represent their moves. The Rock Paper Scissors game has three moves represented by the "Rock," the "Paper," and the "Scissors." The Rock is the move thrown by clenching the fist. The Paper is the move thrown by outstretching your hand. The Scissors is exhibited by using the thumb to hold down the ring finger and pinky while allowing space between the index and middle fingers as they point toward the opponent. However, it should be noted that some moves are being created by people to expand the gameplay of the RPS game. These new moves are either prohibited by the authorities of the RPS game or largely restricted as they can alter the entire face of the game.

The RPS game continues to thrive as it fulfills the purpose for which it is created. With this realization, one thing comes to mind. That is, something must have been guiding the game as it continues to be played by many. A game is only successful if it does not lose its value in the eyes of the players. The question simply is, what has made the RPS game a valued game among people? How does the game increasingly garner interest from different people while sticking to its objectives? The answers to these questions would lay bare the reason the game has not stopped fulfilling the desires of the people interested in the game.

It is straightforward enough to conclude that the rules and regulations of the RPS game have helped it since its discovery. You can agree that there are rules of engagement for every game that allows the participant to do and avoid doing certain things. These rules of engagement are not there to hinder the participant from winning but are given to direct and guide him into winning. Essentially, the rules of the game will lead the participant into the fulfillment of the purpose of the game. Without the rules, you cannot know what to do or what not to do. If you think the RPS game has existed for so long, it is simply because the rules guiding the game are intact and still practiced. This is why the authorities of the RPS game are doing everything within their capacity to see to it that the rules are not bent by allowing other moves classified as illegal to permeate the system.

The rules created for the game cut across the conduct of players, management of the game, procedures of play, calculation moves, etc. The rules are the parts that make up the engine room of the game. Whether you are just getting to know about the RPS game or you wish to have background knowledge of the game, knowing these rules will offer you more understanding of the game and how it is being managed.

The Hand Gestures

The RPS game has three major throws or moves apart from any other illegal moves you may later encounter. The moves are the Rock, Paper, and Scissors. These three hand signals have been endorsed to ensure uniformity of practice. These moves have been approved for both professional and informal play. It is advisable to learn the signals and know how to move your hand, particularly to prevent your opponent from being aware of your intended throw.

The RPS application

The simple rules that guide the interpretation of the Rock, Paper, and Scissors moves are as follows: Rock beats Scissors, Scissors beats Paper, and Paper beats Rock. This is how every move you throw will be interpreted, and the rule is the generally accepted analysis of the moves. You may use a combination of these throws at any time during the match.

Illegal Throws

The Rock, Paper, and Scissors are only the recognized throws. Every participant, especially in a regulated tournament, must be aware of this rule. It is no doubt that illegal and other non-sanctioned moves continue to surface in a bid to expand the game. The authorities, however, are working against any move to change the face of the game. Any other throw like Dynamite, Bird, Water, Fire, God, Devil, etc. will attract automatic disqualification. An illegal throw can be used to confuse the opponent. Participants must be aware of this trick.

Eligibility For Professional Games

For any interested person to be allowed to participate in a professional tournament, it is unnecessary to be a member of the World RPS Association or possess any official status in the RPS system.

Throw Deliveries

There should not be any case of dire physical contact of the fists that can cause scrapping or cut in the process of making a throw. It would be best if you exercise caution and dexterity in this regard as it could be termed as intention harming the opponent.

Verbal Prompts Or Gestures

The spectators and trainers are not expected to make any gesture or verbal presentation that may be of assistance to the participants during the game. Failure to comply attracts disqualification.

Discretion To End

There is usually no limit as to the number of games that can be played. It is left to the discretion of the participants either to continue or stop at their own mutual agreement. Every decision reached in the course of playing is considered a mutual intent of both parties.

THE OFFICIAL RULES OF ROCK PAPER SCISSORS

Tournament Format

This will be a single-elimination tournament, best-of-five series to win. The first contestant to win three games shall be considered the winner of the match.

The Setup of the Game

Before the game starts, the players must agree upon what decision is to be made (and considered binding) as a result of the match. If no compromise or agreement could be struck and the players still wish to continue, then the match by default is considered to be an "honor" match.

The number of primes (draws) to be used is four. An audible counting of the primes "1, 2, 3, shoot" may be used by the players. In recreational games alterations of this may be made and must be agreed upon between the two players.

The decision-makers must stand opposite each other, with one outstretched fist at waist height, with a distance between their fists of no less than 1 foot and no more than 4 feet.

In recreational games the players must agree on the number of rounds to be played before the match is concluded. If they can't reach an agreement on this, the game by default will be a single-round format. Card-carrying WRPSA members are able to determine the number of rounds in a match of RPS before a match and it is considered to be binding (i.e., best of 3, best of 5, best of 161, etc.). The Card must be shown prior to play. For tournament play the number of rounds must be clearly stated by the referee.

Beginning the Play—Pre-Prime Phase

A "call for prime" is issued by one player to his/her opponent in a RAT (recognizable audible tone). A Recognizable Audible Tone is defined as an utterance that can be heard by the challenging player. Using the word "ready" is considered good form.

In the case of a match with or between hearing-impared players or in situations where it is critical that silence must be maintained, a mutually agreement upon Recognizable Visual Signal (RVS) can replace the standard RAT. In this case, a nod of the head while looking directly into the eyes of the other player is accepted as the standard form.

A "return of the call" is then issued by the other player, who thus acknowledges the "call for prime," also in a RVS (or RAT). Once the "return of the call" has been established, players are considered to be "at ready."

Play may begin anytime after the players are established and recognized as being "at ready."

The Game is considered to be "in play" after any player "breaks ready" and thus "initiates the prime."

Priming

The vertical prime is performed by retracting the outstretched fist back towards the player's shoulder (players must face each other and perform the prime with arms parallel).

The fist should be retracted towards the player's own body rather than your opponent's to avoid possible contact.

As soon as one player has "broken ready" and initiated the first prime, it is the responsibility and obligation of the opponent also to begin priming and to "sync" or "catch" the prime with the first player so they can establish a delivery and approach.

The player who has initiated the prime is under the strict obligation to maintain a constant priming speed so as to give his opponent every opportunity to "catch the prime."

The fist must remain in the closed position until the delivery of the final prime. The fist is the only acceptable hand position during the prime.

The fist must remain in full view of the opposing player and may not come in contact with any outside influences that inhibit the opponent's view.

Before the delivery of the final prime, the game may be called off for the following reasons only: decision clarification, rule clarification, or injury.

Approach

Once the fist has reached the highest point of the final throw of the last prime, the delivery of the throw is considered to be "in approach." At anytime during the approach of this final prime, the hand may be released in any of the following manners:

Rock: Represented by a closed fist with the thumb resting at least at the same height as the topmost finger of the hand. The thumb must not be concealed by the fingers.

Note: To accommodate different throwing styles, it is considered legal for the first knuckle of the thumb to point downward.

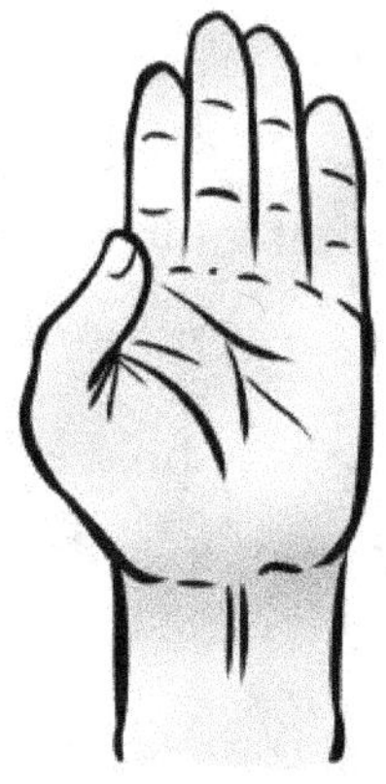

Paper: Is also delivered in the same manner as Rock with the exception that all fingers including the thumb are fully extended and horizontal with the points of the fingers facing the opposing player. Use of the "vertical paper" (sometimes referred to as "the handshake") is considered a professional approach.

Scissors: Is delivered in the same manner as Rock with the exception that the index and middle fingers are fully extended toward the opposing player. It is considered good form to angle the topmost finger upwards and the lower finger downwards in order to create a roughly 30-45-degree angle between the two digits and thus mimic a pair of scissors.

Throws must be delivered prior to the completion of the approach. The approach is considered finished when the forearm is at a 90-degree angle to the upper body. Any throw not delivered prior to the hand crossing the 90-degree mark shall be considered a throw of Rock.

Delivery

Participants must exercise extreme caution, dexterity, and care not to initiate contact between the opposing fists during any point of the priming phase. The direct contact of the fists can cause chaffing, scraping, or rapping of the knuckles. Make sure any onlookers are aware of the intentions of the players as the swinging of closed fists can be mistaken as a sign of a potentially combative situation.

Should direct contact occur, players should stop play immediately and assess if there are any personal injuries before restarting the prime.

After players have revealed their throws, play must stop until an agreement can be reached as to a winner or if a stalemate situation has arisen.

Throws

A game of Rock Paper Scissors can have only the following outcomes.

Rock wins against Scissors

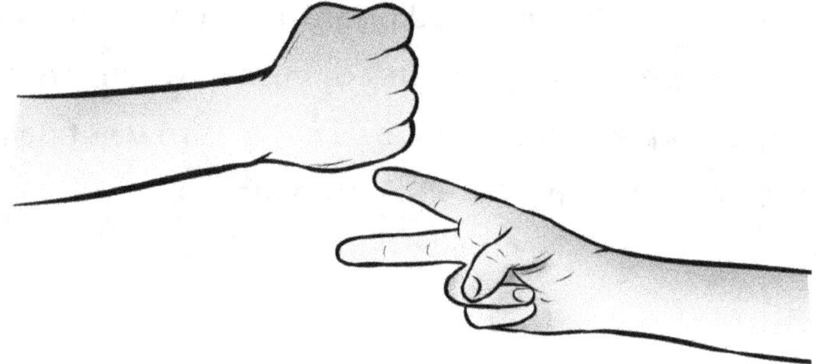

Rock loses to Paper

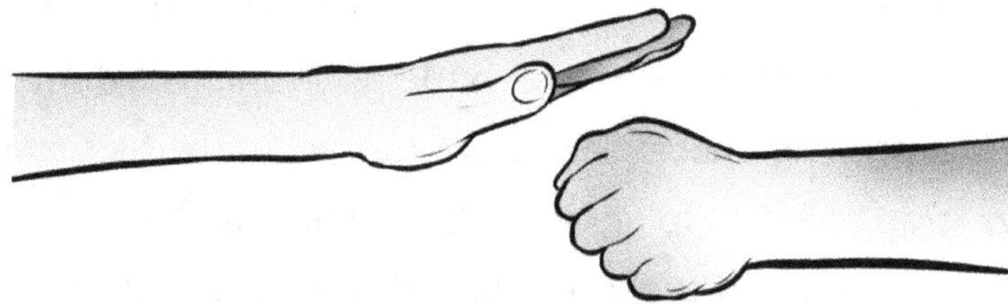

Rock ties against itself

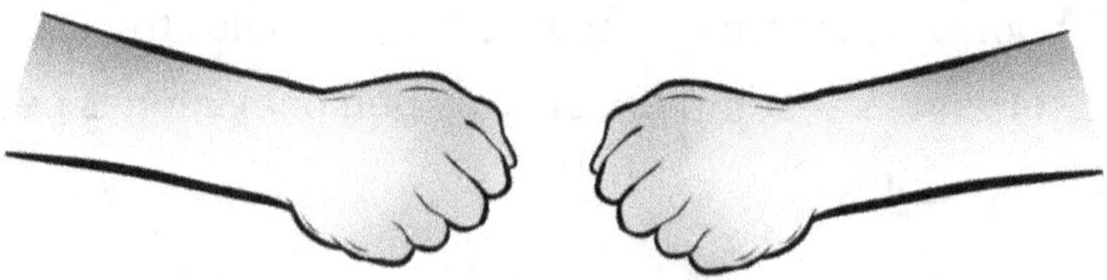

Paper wins against Rock

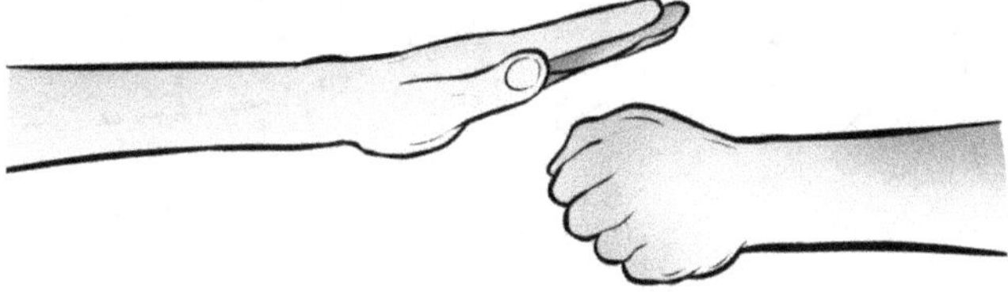

Paper loses to Scissors

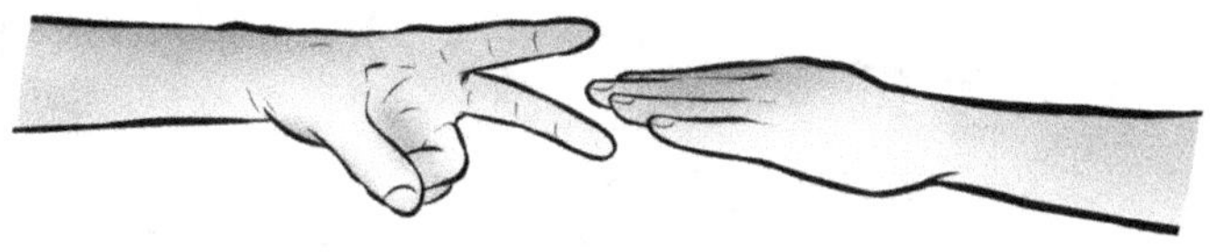

Paper ties against itself

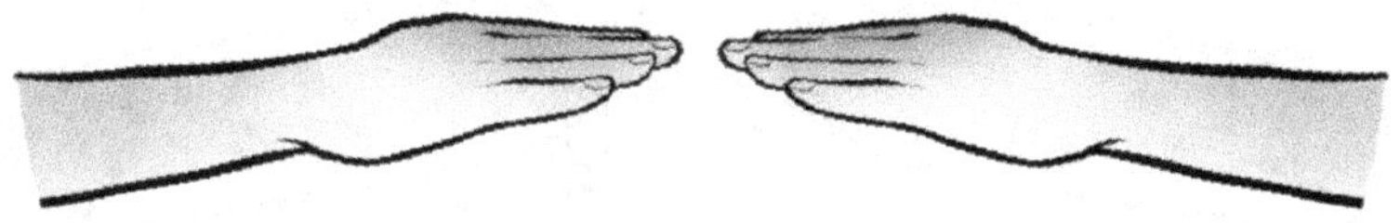

Scissors wins against Paper

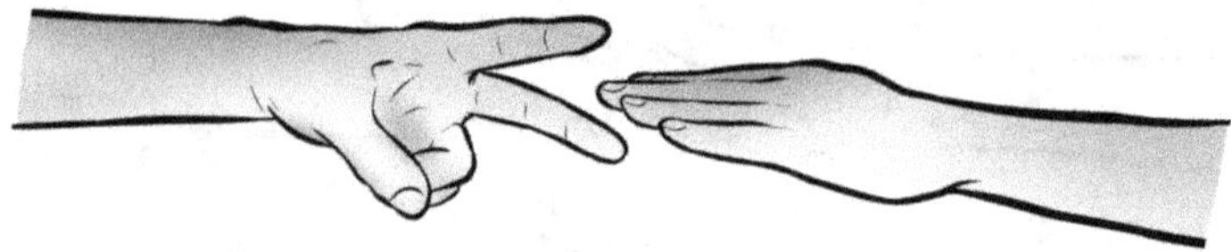

Scissors loses to Rock

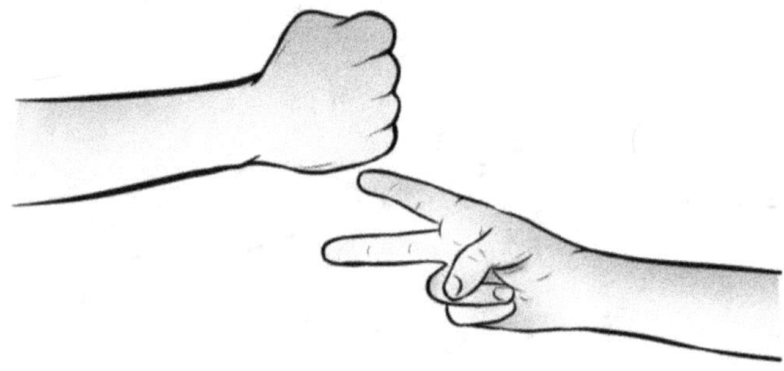

Scissors ties against itself

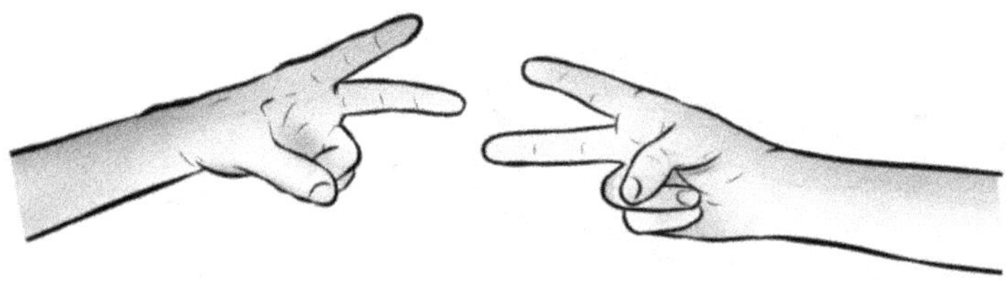

Players may use any combination of these throws at any time throughout the match. Any throws that are not conforming to the standard hand positions (outlined above) and thus deemed to be a Rock (stone), Paper, or Scissors is considered to be an illegal throw and it is forbidden. Should a player execute an illegal throw, the opposing player has the right (but not the obligation) to claim immediate victory over the round (not the match). Alternatively, the infringed upon player has the right but not the obligation to replay the current game if he/she so chooses.

The winner of the round is dictated by the player's throw which beats that of the opponent. Under no circumstances can a losing throw ever beat a winning throw.

In the case of a stalemate, where players reveal the same throw, the round must be replayed. There are no limits to the numbers of stalemates which may occour in any given match. Should players find themselves in a continuous stalemate situation, also known as "Mirror Play," a good approach can be to take a short "timeout" to rethink your strategy.

Post-Game Play

There is no limit to the number of rounds, matches, or games that can be played in RPS. The game may continue until any and all decisions are reached and is at the discretion of the players involved. Games for honor can be substituted at any point after the conclusion of a match as long as it is agreed upon by all players involved before the beginning of the next match.

THE PRIMING PHASE IN ROCK PAPER SCISSORS

The Rock Paper Scissors game, like any other game, has a planning phase. Apart from the preparations RPS tournaments organizers are expected to make, there are some other arrangements that the players themselves should make for their own benefit. This priming phase has almost if not already become an essential part of the process of winning an RPS game. This article will exhaustively discuss those things that must be settled and taken care of in the priming phase before an RPS game. It should be noted that this planning is geared toward helping the player in one way or the other.

Embracing The Atmosphere Of The Venue

The venue has an influence on a player's preparedness. It contains some of those things that must be effectively dealt with before the match. One is that the player does not want to feel strange in the venue and at the same time, he wants to have control of everything that goes on around him during the match. If this is the case, then he must do these three things before the match.

The Pre-Match Sight

It is ideal to get to the venue of the match hours before. This is to allow the player the time to survey the venue and get acquainted with the atmosphere of the place. He needs to take it all in. There is a psychological effect to this. It makes the player aware of his environment and become conscious. More importantly, it helps boost confidence levels. It is advisable for an RPS player to get settled and comfortable in the venue before the match. The body is able to adapt to the venue, and the mind is well-rested too.

Find A Comfortable Locker Room Before The Match

In the course of settling in before the match, the player, while surveying the venue, may seek the locker room that he wants to stay during the game. Although this is not essential, it helps the player gain build control over his game as his confidence is increased by being in a place where he feels comfortable and at ease. Again, this is psychological.

Handle The Crowd

Whether the player likes it or not, the crowd has come to stay in every RPS game. Spectators are allowed into the venue to witness the game and show support for their favorite players or throws. Of course, they are acting within the confines of the RPS regulations and will not be denied entrance as long as they do not try to influence the game or perpetrate any form of cheating. However, the raving atmosphere may alter the concentration of the players. It is left to every player to practice mindfulness and ensure that he is not distracted by the shouts and roars.

Act Professional Even If You Are Not

The truth is that the Rock Paper Scissors game requires professionalism. Yes, beginners may try their luck, but without some certain level of experience and skill, they cannot go far in the game. This is organizers for RPS tournaments are always trying to ensure that only professional players are enrolled. Although, doing this does not give the assurance that a player will act professionally as the case may be, however, it does signify that any player in the tournament must at least have a strong grip of the game. One of the preparations a player should make is to act professionally before and during the game.

The way you approach the venue, how you carry yourself, and the way you act are all signals that can be read. Should an opponent sense that a player appears like a novice, he might become aggressive to unease and intimidate that player. A player should carry himself as though he is at the same level or even better than his opponent even if he is not. It is simple, fake it till you become it.

Handle Yourself

Self-management is one of the crucial factors that will help you define the game when it is being played. As a player who wants to get hold of the match, handle your opponent, and get the best out of the game, you must be ready to activate some things in yourself. These things will not only help you build up yourself with the necessary knowledge you need for the match, but it will also boost your confidence, morale, and ultimately your chances of winning.

Don't Be Swayed By The Opponent.

Part of the preparations a player needs to make in the process of handling himself is to learn to be unmoved by his opponent. This is especially true in pre-match meetings or conferences where some aggressive opponents may throw offensive remarks or try to intimidate the other players. Some opponents may even try to mislead the other player by talking about a move. For instance, a player may say to the public that "Rocks are for beginners." Upon hearing this, the opponent may think Rock will come in handy but may not know that he was being tricked into thinking the former will not fancy throwing Rock. He is sure to end up in the cold hands of Paper. In essence, a player must learn not to be moved or intimidated by his opponent at any point.

Master Your Strategies

Before the match, an RPS player needs to go over his strategies again and again in order to perfect his preparations. This will help him master his throws. In the process, he may be able to develop and set aside a series of strategic throws to save himself in the moment of disaster. Mastering strategies will help the player stay focused and unmoved by any form of distractions.

Study Your Opponent

In most professional tournaments, players take their time to watch their opponents' previous games. The essence of this is to learn how the opponent reads his game and execute his strategies. By doing this, the player is able to take careful notice of his opponent's movement. In crucial and deciding moments, what the player has gained from watching his opponent play may just be what would save him. If a player wants to be able to handle his opponent, he must learn his moves and strikes him when and where he seems weak. As the player reads his opponent, he can organize his strategies against the opponent and carry them out without delay or frustration.

Be Mindful, Always

This cannot be underestimated in the RPS game. The game is a psychological game, and that means a player's mind must be in the game at all times. Whether it is before or during the game, mindfulness is everything to a player's level of preparedness. A player who intends to control the game and win his opponent should always have his mind in the game. He should not consider the tense atmosphere, raving spectators, or the tricks to unease him by his opponent. A player that loses his mind will lose the game.

Never Rely On Cheating

The rules of the RPS game do not in any way condone any form of cheating. As a result, there are strict regulations against trying to manipulate the game in favour of one against the other. Cheating can be perpetrated by the players themselves, by the referee, or by a spectator conniving with any of the players. However, it is the players that are usually found in the cases of cheating. As a result of the strong position of the RPS authorities against cheating, disqualification has been the quick and instant punishment meted out on players discovered to have cheated during the game. For players, cheating can be throwing illegal moves, frequent delay of throws, or speaking derogatory remarks against an opponent during the game.

Trust The Referee With Your Score

As a player, it is usually difficult to keep track of the score. This is because the mind is focused on the game and could be distracted by trying to remember the score. Therefore, the only person that can accurately keep the score is the referee in charge of the game. The player needs not to disturb himself by trying to do the job of the referee or exhibiting doubts as to the credibility of the referee in keeping score. Doing this may ultimately distract him. A professional RPS player who wants to win should concentrate on the game and trust the referee to keep his score straight and accurate.

Skillset Is Not Enough, Hope For Luck

Two things are complementary to each other in the Rock Paper Scissors game. They are skill and luck. If you have ever heard an RPS player lamenting he had a bad match despite having the skill, luck must have been far from him. In the same way, a player cannot rely on luck only. It is dangerous that way. We can say luck is when preparation meets opportunity. In other words, luck can only come to aid when the player has everything else under control. A player should be confident about his abilities before the game. As long as he has the skill, he can improve on his gameplay during the game. Eventually, luck might just smile on him.

DESCRIPTIONS OF MOVES IN ROCK PAPER SCISSORS

The game of Rock Paper Scissors comes with a very unique form. Its uniqueness is evident in its general outlook, although it also sums up the fact that it is complex. The complexities that surround the Rock Paper Scissors game can be seen in the gameplay, calculations, as well as the interpretations that are involved. Also, the fact that the game involves psychology cannot be underplayed. This is one of the sure realities of the Rock Paper Scissors game; the game is a psychological game. Perhaps it is due to this plus many other reasons that the Rock Paper Scissors game is termed complex and completely different from most games or sports you will see around.

One of the crucial and irremovable elements of the Rock Paper Scissors game is the plays of the game. Although it looks simple and straightforward, the interpretation of each of the plays is essential for the fulfillment of the purpose of the game. The knowledge of these plays, their calculations, and interpretations are, therefore, part of what is required to master the game. Thus, the more reason why the game is confirmed complex. Whatever the case may be, though, the fact that the Rock Paper Scissors game puts up a complex face does not mean one cannot understand the fundamentals of the game. This is what this article will seek to achieve; to offer detailed explanations of the plays that are involved in the RPS game.

These plays are simply the basic elements of the game. They are the reason why the game bears its name. They cannot be changed or removed as they are the face of the game. We can even affirm that these elements are the game itself, and without them, RPS cannot stand. However, since the development of the game, there have been a series of unwelcome moves to change the face of the game by adding and/or removing some of the elements. The truth is that any modification of these elements will alter the nature game and possibly defeat the purpose of why the game was created. However, the good news is that deliberate altering or modification of the Rock Paper Scissors game has not been successful. The original and true nature of the RPS game is still being preserved, probably due to the active measures, rules, and regulations created by the RPS authorities.

One thing that is worthy of note is that the elements that will be discussed in this article cannot be substituted or removed from the game. They form the general outlook of the game and essentially indicate why the game is what it is. It is, therefore, important that these elements should be understood in order to strengthen one's knowledge of the game. It is simple. If you want to master the game, learn these elements, for, without them, there is no Rock Paper Scissors game. As we go into the explanation now, take note of the interpretations of the elements and particularly how they relate with one another. This knowledge is crucial if you want to improve your professionalism in the game.

The Three Generally Accepted Moves

In the Rock Paper Scissors game, ever since its inception, only three moves have been certified as the only legal and accepted move in the game. This simply identifies any other move as illegal. These three moves have continued to be the only moves that can be related to the Rock Paper Scissors game. What is more interesting is the fact that the three moves are used to name the game itself. The name of the game is the exact representation of the three moves. Do you see why the moves cannot be changed or removed?

These three moves can also be referred to as throws. They are hand gestures extended by the player. And only one move or hand gesture can be thrown at a time. You know how the RPS game is played, right? Two players throw a series of moves against one another to see whose throws or moves can win over the other. These moves are then interpreted and calculated according to their interpretations. We will get to their calculations later. The three moves have their significance in the game and also their features. Forming the major part of the game, the moves or throws carry a huge responsibility to deliver the purpose of the game. Now, let us consider the three moves that are generally accepted in the Rock Paper Scissors game.

Rock

Rock sometimes referred to as stone one of the three moves. The characteristics of rock are also transferred to the object in the RPS game. For instance, a rock or stone can be used to crush something. In the Rock Paper Scissors game, Rock is represented by a fist. That is, the player closes his fist and extends the gesture toward the opponent. This represents a play and a part of the elements of the game.

Paper

Paper is the second of the elements of the game. The identity of Paper in the game is also the same as the paper you have in the bookshelf. Therefore, RPS's Paper carries the same characteristics. For instance, the paper is a flat piece that can be used to wrap an object. In the Rock Paper Scissors game, Paper is a hand gesture, represented by extending a flat palm toward the opponent. Just as if you want to extend a handshake.

Scissors

Scissors is the last, though, not the least of the three moves that form the basic elements of the RPS game. As usual, Scissors in Rock Paper Scissors game is the same as the scissors used in the house. Thus, the RPS's Scissors carries the same characteristics as the scissors you can find around. For instance, Scissors is used for cutting or decrease an object. In the Rock Paper Scissors game,

Scissors is a hand gesture represented by forming scissors with your hand. Here, the player holds down his ring finger and pinky down with his thumb while extending the index and middle fingers to form the "V" shape. The "V" shape is similar to forming the "victory" hand sign. The difference is just that the "V" in "victory" gesture is raised upward while the Scissors throw is toward the opponent.

The Triangle Relationship Between the Three Moves

You may be surprised how a game would be represented by objects as above and having the same characteristics as the original objects. Do not be surprised just yet. Wait till you see how they are interpreted in the Rock Paper Scissors game. The relationship between the three moves is a very interesting one. Three of them are connected one way or another. Consider the shape of a triangle. Each of the angles is connected to the two other angles. Also, just like the lines to the two other angles are different, the relationship between the angle and each of the two other angles are as well different.

To put it more simply, the connections between one angle and the other two are different. One may be said to be above the angle while the other is below it. An interpretation of this connection in the RPS game will be that one move scares one of the other moves but is afraid of the second move. You will get it better as we calculate the connection each of the moves has on one another.

Rock beats Scissors but gets beaten by Paper.

The interpretation for this throw is that Rock will crush Scissors as it can be realistically practiced by smashing a stone against scissors. However, Rock cannot handle Paper as Paper will wrap itself around Rock (to suffocate it). The identity of Rock as either small or big is not given here, but at least we get the idea of suffocating.

Paper beats Rock but gets beaten by Scissors.

We said earlier that Paper would wrap itself around Rock to suffocate it. However, Paper is also scared of Scissors. It should be. By calculation, Paper is at the risk of being turned to pieces by Scissors.

Scissors beats Paper but gets beaten by Rock.

Paper is at the mercy of Scissors, but Scissors must also run from the big hand of Rock.

Have you seen the awesome calculations of the moves in the Rock Paper Scissors game? Their relationship is such that one is a master to one but a slave to another. For instance, if A beats B, B will beat C, and C will beat A. These are the three moves recognized in a formal and regulated Rock Paper Scissors game like RPS tournaments. The rules and regulations that guide the RPS game continue to protect it against a couple of other moves that some people have tried to add to the game's original moves. In essence, if you wish to master the game, you must first learn these three moves explained in this article and understand how each throw is calculated.

ROCK PAPER SCISSORS PSYCHOLOGY

Every sport or game involves mindfulness to some extent. It is only the levels that appear different. The level of mindfulness that you put into playing tennis is definitely different from that of boxing. As far as playing the Rock Paper Scissors game is concerned, we are talking about mindfulness on a different level entirely. Any random person who has witnessed players playing RPS games can testify to the kind of atmosphere that is experienced. The players even understand what mindfulness is and would quickly come to terms with the fact that mindfulness is one of the crucial aspects of learning the game.

One of the truths associated with the fact that mindfulness strongly exists in the Rock Paper Scissors game can be traced back to the origin of the game. There is no doubt that old Asia has a flair for human psychology. Many of their activities are built upon the idea of meditation and the mind. The Rock Paper Scissors game is not any different. Since its creation even, the RPS game has continued to exhibit human consciousness as one of its predominant characteristics. It is therefore correct to assert that the Rock Paper Scissors game has a lot to do with the player's mind.

In this article, we will discuss the psychology that is contained in the Rock Paper Scissors game and how it influences the game. Also, we will talk about how you can build and sustain your mindfulness in a way that gives you control of the game while you balance both your physical actions (hand gestures) and mental processes. Combining all these, you will be able to gain the insights necessary for you to improve your gameplay, skills, and concentration levels.

The Psychology Of The Game

The Rock Paper Scissors game has in it a combination of both physical and mental exertions that every player must be ready to give. The addition of both the physical and mental efforts is what makes the game pleasurable and as well enjoyable to play. At the same time, offering both physical and mental requirements of the game will help you master the art of the game, play well, and eventually gives you dominance over your opponent. This is simply to tell you that as much as physical exertions like mastery of the hand gestures and body movements are not the only thing that can win you're the game. Mental processes like building consciousness and mindreading are also important skills you must develop in order to complete your professional training.

In other words, there is a balance that should be made between your body and your mind as far as the Rock Paper Scissors is concerned. In any case that there is no balance or either of the elements is absent, you may not enjoy the game and end up losing. For instance, a player that has mastered all the hand gestures and formed possible winning strategies but lacks the mental preparedness is likely to lose the match for lack of concentration. In the same way, mental preparedness will not help you much if you have no dexterity.

What we are trying to say here is that your mental condition before and during the Rock Paper Scissors game is crucial and an additional factor that can aid your performance. Essentially, psychology predicts winning or losing. It is extremely difficult for a player who lacks consciousness or in a disturbed mood to concentrate on the game he is playing. Even so, the world RPS trainers usually sensitize their players on human psychology before tournaments in order to help them prepare mentally for their matches.

How The Mind Influences The Game

There is no doubt that the mind influences the Rock Paper Scissors game. The mental conditions of the players in the game directly influence the players' performance. To measure the level of influence, consider the performance of a player when he is in a bad mood. In such a case, the player is likely to be aggressive, passive, lack concentration, and unaware of his opponent as he is not able to read the game as he should. Such a player may throw the wrong moves leading to his quick elimination from the match. Here, the problem is not the level of experience that he has but the state of mind. His mental state has altered his actions, reactions, and concentration in the game.

In the same way that an impaired mental condition can affect the player's performance, so also can a positive mindset. When the mind of the player is balanced and well relaxed, he will be able to concentrate on his game and also monitor the moves of the opponent. His mental condition will not only improve his gameplay but also help maintain good composure when it comes to reacting and making move choices.

Practicing And Sustaining Mindfulness

Improving one's psychology in the Rock Paper Scissors game is a crucial task that every player should be interested in. The task of building a positive mindset before and maintaining it during the game is not easy, but you will eventually get a hold of it. Practice makes perfection. The more you practice mindfulness, the better you get at building a positive mindset.

Also, it should be noted that building and sustaining a positive mindset for RPS games should be a deliberate effort. First, you need to develop an interest in building up your mental state. This should be balanced with the physical practice that involves mastering the hand gestures. The combination of an improved skill set and a positive mental state builds a powerful force that can break through the strategies of your opponent.

human psychology is an exciting aspect of the Rock Paper Scissors game. Various studies have been taken in order to discover the extent to which the mind operates when it comes to performance in RPS matches. This is what this article has discussed in the simplest yet understandable way. This should help you understand the necessity to build the mental state in preparation for RPS games.

WHAT YOUR MOVE IN ROCK PAPER SCISSORS SAYS ABOUT YOU

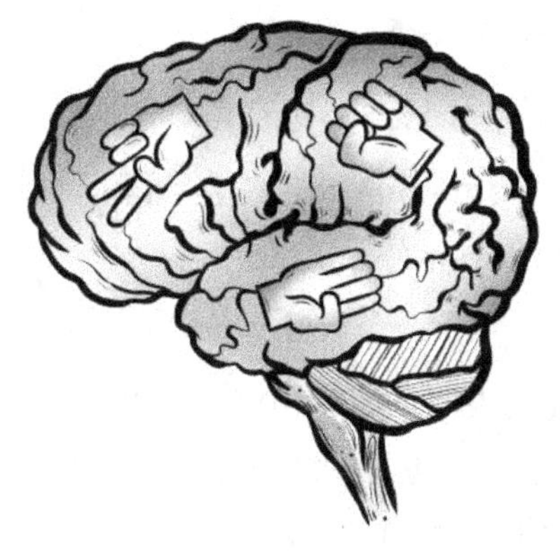

The Rock Paper Scissors game has a lot of interesting features. These features make up the unique nature of the game, as well as the complexities that can be found therein. This is especially true when it comes to discussing the form or nature of the game. For anyone trying to get a grasp of what the Rock Paper Scissors game is all about, he is sure to encounter the complexities that surround it in the course of learning. However, this is not to say that the game will be extremely difficult to learn or master. You will be surprised how easy it is for anyone to understand the basics of the RPS game as long as you take your time and open your mind to learn it.

In the actual sense, it is the complexities of the RPS game that make it such a fascinating game to play. An interesting nature of the game is that it involves your physical presence and your undivided mental presence. The RPS game, as you already know, requires your hand movements. Also, it requires that you are actively conscious, and your mind is aware of what is going on. This is one of the features of the game that not many people have realized. Although some games or sports may also require your mindfulness, however, you cannot compare the expected level of mindfulness with what is required in the Rock Paper Scissors game.

How The Mind Connects With Your Moves

Perhaps we can conclude that the mind is one of the powerful forces behind the game. Apart from your ability to make throws, your mind is expected to be at optimal condition. It is simple. Whatever move you make with your hand, your mind must have run the processes. Without the active participation of your brain or mind in the Rock Paper Scissors game, you cannot go far. In essence, you need the support of your mind so that you can be able to handle the game like a pro and ultimately enjoy playing to get the best out of it.

In order words, the mental process is one of the complexities of the Rock Paper Scissors game. Without it, your moves, calculations, and interpretations are likely to fail. You cannot go far in the game without the active use of your mind. The psychology feature that is embedded in the RPS game makes the game an interesting topic of research. Over the years, sports enthusiasts and interested persons have devoted their time and resources to the study of how the mind is put to work the Rock Paper Scissors game. From their studies and outcomes, there have been various revelations beyond what was even expected.

Different theories on how the mind is connected to the Rock Paper Scissors game have been explained in order to widen the scope of the understanding of the game. By taking the time to study the kind of relationship that exists between the human mind and the game, one will be able to understand how to leverage the chances discovered therein. That is correct. There are a lot of chances of winning if you can only actively engage your mind while playing the game. Nonetheless, of these possibilities, you may get nothing out of it if you do not understand how it works and how you can practice it.

Having understood that, we can now move further on this discussion. The Rock Paper Scissors game is not an ordinary game seeing its strong connection with the mind. That has been settled. At this point, it is important to let you know that your mind that processes a move or throw before you extend your hand gesture is trying to tell you something about yourself. Do you know that? Many people do not. The choices of throws you make, whether you are playing just a match or series of rounds, are the interpretations of the kind of person you are, either at that moment of playing or in your everyday life. This is what this article will exhaustively discuss.

The conclusion now is that the mind works in mysterious ways. It interprets something about you by sending a signal to your brain. The interpretation is then completed when you extend your throw. You must have heard the popular statement that "as a man thinketh, so is he." This is exactly what we are talking about. The moves you make in the Rock Paper Scissors game are saying something about you because they are triggered by your mind.

Now, before we try to explain what these moves say about your person, it is essential to clearly lay out the moves in Rock Paper Scissors, their features, and what they entail. This is to help us connect the dot between what your mind is trying to interpret and what each of the moves means. That is, for every move you make, you are expressing something about yourself. If we can identify the features of the move, then we can conclude what the mind is trying to interpret. Remember, the moves can talk.

The Three Throws And Their Features

In the Rock Paper Scissors game, there are three universally accepted moves, and each has distinct features and interpretations. Let us consider them.

Rock: The Rock move is expressed by extending a fist toward the opponent. Like the usual rock, some of the qualities of a Rock include weight, solidity, and roughness, among others. The interpretation of throwing Rock in the game is that it crushes scissors.

Paper: Paper is flat and is gestured by extending a flat palm toward the opponent. The notable features include smoothness and its usefulness in wrapping objects. In the game, Paper covers Rock.

Scissors: This is represented by forming a "V" shape with the index and middle fingers while holding down the pinky and ring finger with the thumb. The major features that Scissors possess are sharpness and the ability to cut through something, thus making Paper prey.

The Descriptions Of Each Move In Rock Paper Scissors

It will be easy for us to discover the hidden interpretations of every move since we can understand their relevance in the game. Now let us discuss what each throw in the Rock Paper Scissors game says about the thrower.

What Rock Says

Rock is unarguably regarded as the most aggressive among the throws. It identifies with the images of tall and heavy mountains and the stone axe of cavemen. More often than not, players unconsciously fall back on using Rock as protection when the other strategies appear to fail them. Apart from being the most aggressive, it is also the easiest to throw. It takes the position of being the commonest throw among RPS beginners. Perhaps due to its perceived size, Rock is easily associated with players who are trying to intimidate their opponents. A careless throw of Scissors may be a sweet offering for the crushing Rock. Let see what Rock says about the thrower:

Rock identifies the thrower as overconfident and overbearing to the point of being arrogant.

It shows that the thrower is aggressive and looking for a quick win.

Rock creates a straightforward and blunt intention. I.e., a deliberate plan to throw.

It displays the thrower to be powerful and stronger than the opponent.

What Paper Says

Due to the creation of this throw, it is the least throw expected to be an opening throw. Although one trick is that since Rock is usually likely to be an opening throw, a risky throw of Paper will effortlessly deal with the big hand. A piece of paper is harmless, making Paper a cool throw. The gesture itself explains a lot. Extending an open palm is a sign of friendship and peace. What does Paper say about the thrower?

Paper says that the thrower is trying to monitor the game at first, making him conserves his strength.

Paper calls the thrower timid. This makes him to be protective in his throws. A player that feels threatened by his opponent is more likely to throw Paper.

The throw shows that the thrower is trying to weigh his options, thus making him open-minded.

It suggests that the thrower is weak in his thought and may want to preserve his scores by always targeting Rock.

What Scissors Says

Scissors is a tool used for cutting or opening objects and packages. That means its use comes with a little bit of aggression, although not the same as Rock. Scissors is often used for carefully planned act, thus making the throw controlled and constructive. See what Scissors says about you:

Scissors shows the thrower is not afraid of the opponent, even if he throws Rock.

The throw calls the thrower reactive as it makes you understand your opponent and change your tactics at any point. Yes, Scissors will make you calculate the game better.

Scissors shows you are calm. If you want to cut an object or open a box using scissors, you sure have to be careful with it to cut perfectly.

Scissors shows you are cunning and waiting for an opportunity. If you thought you could suffocate Rock by throwing Paper, you have just prepared a sweet meal for Scissors.

HOW TO WIN AT ROCK PAPER SCISSORS

If you see someone who has always won the Rock Paper Scissors as being lucky, I think you need to have a rethink. It goes beyond being lucky as there are known techniques that can guarantee a consistent winning streak. I will be talking about some of this technique here.

In fact, consistently winning at Rock, Paper, Scissors only requires reading through a bit of strategy, and you'll be ready to win every challenge and throw. It is all about strategy

If your opponent loses to you on the first throw, then it becomes easy to predict their next move due to that human tendency towards conditional responses. It is normal for everybody.

The reason for this is because people are influenced by the choices they have previously made. If the previous choice did not work, it is always a natural tendency to try another choice.

One of the fundamentally known techniques to winning Rock Paper Scissors is to pay attention to your opponent's choices, and your chances of emerging a winner automatically increase.

There is no sure way to guarantee that you will win throw one, so just keep it simple: throw paper. Unless your opponent is also trained in the art of winning Rock Paper Scissors, you should have a better chance of winning because people choose to throw rock first more often than paper or scissors. If you've won the first round, great. You're on your way to victory.

What did your opponent throw on the first hand?

Whatever it was, choose the next item in the rotation of Rock - Paper - Scissors. People typically move through these three choices in order and are also very unlikely to repeat their losing choice. So, if your opponent chose paper, they will probably throw scissors next.

So, you should choose rock. If they chose scissors, they would probably choose rock, so you should choose paper.

If you lost the first round, don't panic. There's still hope. When someone wins, they're more likely to pick the same thing again because they feel that it was a good choice.

Remember this important rule about your opponent; if they won with scissors, you should pick rock to win the next throw, because chances are, they will pick scissors again. Remember this rule, and you will your chances of winning is higher.

Follow these three rules for playing the game, and your chances of winning Rock, Paper, Scissors will be high enough for you to take over the role as the "Lucky Friend" without anyone ever realizing how you did it.

The first throw: Men tend to pick rock as their first throw, maybe because rocks are more of a stereotypically masculine symbol.

Women usually throw paper first. So if you're playing against a man, you should throw paper first; if you are playing with a woman, throw scissors.

After the first loss: Once someone loses a round, they don't throw the same thing they just threw immediately after. In fact, they often throw the thing that beat them.

If someone lost by throwing a rock against paper, they would probably throw paper next. Knowing that can help you beat someone twice in a row.

A study from China's Zhejiang University found another pattern in what people throw after a loss. The study found a triangle of moves that people throw in order:

If your opponent lost with a rock, they would likely choose paper next. If they lost with paper, they'll choose scissors, and so on.

How to beat a winner: In general, people who win play the winning symbol again directly afterward, according to the Zhejiang University study. If your opponent just beat you with scissors, play rock against them next, because they will likely throw scissors again.

A fun trick: One way to throw people off is to announce what you're about to throw before you throw it; and then follow through. Your opponent won't trust you, and will be expecting you to throw anything other than what you announced.

Contrary to what you might think Rock Paper Scissors is not simply a game of luck or chance. While it is true that from a mathematical perspective the 'optimum' strategy is to play randomly, it still is not a winning strategy for two reasons.

First, 'optimum' in this case means you should win, lose and draw an equal number of times (hardly a winning strategy over the long term).

Second, Humans, try as they might, are terrible at trying to be random, in fact often humans in trying to approximate randomness become quite predictable. Knowing that there is always something motivating your opponent's actions, there are a couple of techniques and tricks that you can use to tip the balance in your favor.

The top secrets to winning at Rock Paper Scissors - are after the jump. So here are a more outlined tactics to follow;

Rock is for Rookies

In RPS circles a common mantra is "Rock is for Rookies" because males have a tendency to lead with Rock on their opening throw. It has a lot to do with idea that Rock is perceived as "strong" and forceful", so guys tend to fall back on it. Use this knowledge to take an easy first win by playing Paper.

Scissors on First

The second step in the 'Rock is for Rookies' line of thinking is to play scissors as your opening move against a more experienced player. Since you know they won't come out with rock (since it is too obvious), scissors is your obvious safe move to win against paper or stalemate to itself.

The Double Run

When playing with someone who is not experienced at the RPS, look out for double runs (the same throw twice). When this happens you can safely eliminate that throw and guarantee yourself at worst a stalemate in the next game. So, when you see a two-Scissor run, you know their next move will be Rock or Paper, so Paper is your best move. Why does this work? People hate being predictable and the perceived hallmark of predictability is to come out with the same throw three times in row.

Telegraph Your Throw

Tell your opponent what you are going to throw and then actually throw what you said. Why? As long as you are not playing someone who actually thinks you are bold enough to telegraph your throw and then actually deliver it, you can eliminate the throw that beats the throw you are telegraphing. So, if you announce rock, your opponent won't play paper which means coming out with that scissors will give you at worst a stalemate and at best the win.

Step Ahead Thinking

Don't know what to do for your next throw? Try playing the throw that would have lost to your opponents last throw? Sounds weird but it works more often than not, why? Inexperienced (or flustered) players will often subconsciously deliver the throw that beat their last one. Therefore, if your opponent played paper, they will very often play Scissors, so you go Rock. This is a good tactic in a stalemate situation or when your opponent lost their last game. It is not as successful after a player has won the last game as they are generally in a more confident state of mind which causes them to be more active in choosing their next throw.

Suggest A Throw

When playing against someone who asks you to remind them about the rules, take the opportunity to subtly "suggest a throw" as you explain to them by physically showing them the throw you want them to play. ie "Paper beats Rock, Rock beats scissors (show scissors), Scissors (show scissors again) beats paper." Believe it or not, when people are not paying attention their subconscious mind will often accept your "suggestion". A very similar technique is used by magicians to get someone to take a specific card from the deck.

When All Else Fails Go With Paper

If you do not have a clue on what to throw next, then go with Paper. Why? Statistically, in competition play, it has been observed that scissors is thrown the least often. Specifically, it gets delivered 29.6% of the time, so it slightly under-indexes against the expected average of 33.33% by 3.73%. Obviously, knowing this only gives you a slight advantage, but in a situation where you just don't know what to do, even a slight edge is better than none at all.

The Rounder's Ploy

This technique seems more like 'cheating'. Hpwever, if you think all that matters is a win for you and you can live with it yourself the next day by defending your actions, then you can use it to get an edge. The way it works is when you suggest a game with your opponent, do not announce the number of rounds you are going to play. Play the first match and if you win, take it is as a win. If you lose, without missing a beat start playing the 'next' round on the assumption that it was a best 2 out of 3. No doubt you will hear protests from your opponent but stay firm and remind them that 'no one plays best of one for a kind of decision that you two are making'. No this devious technique won't guarantee you the win, but it will give you a chance to battle back to even and start again.

ROCK PAPER SCISSORS STRATEGIES

Physical Skills

The basic skills of RPS need no discussion. Most children can be taught to form the three throws with their hands and with a little practice can follow the prime and reveal their chosen throw at the appropriate time.

An advanced RPS player can do more than that. He can use his hands to confuse or deceive an opponent. She can make her opponent believe she is going to throw Rock when she is going to throw scissors.

Cloaking

"Cloaking" is the term used for delaying the unveiling of the throw. Put a little more simply, "Cloaking" is waiting until the last possible second to throw Paper or Scissors. Some players will watch your hands for an indication of which throw you are about to use. By not moving your fingers until the last moment, you can fool such a player into thinking you are throwing Rock. Since a hand-watcher will respond to a well-executed cloak with paper, cloaking Scissors is more useful than cloaking Paper.

Shadowing

Another step beyond cloaking, "shadowing" is pretending to throw one thing, but changing to another at the last possible moment. This is much more difficult and requires great care in execution. Ultimately, it is up to the judges or referee to decide when that last possible moment arrives and if your hand is on the wrong throw or between throws, they are not very forgiving. There are two primary ways in which you can use shadowing. The first is to twitch your fingers during the prime merely. A hand-watching opponent may believe this to foreshadow a throw of paper or scissors, depending on which fingers you wiggle. A more advanced method of shadowing is to change the position of your hand three or four times during the last prime. This has the possibility of distracting any opponent and will likely befuddle a hand-watcher completely.

Smoothing Tells

"Tells" are visible behaviors through which a player may unconsciously reveal a throw to an opponent. Everyone has them to some degree – they've been the poker player's friend and enemy for centuries. They are the reason that hand-watchers watch hands, but tells aren't always in the hands. The face and lips are common places to find tells. Records from a tournament in 1923 mention a player who wiggled his toes before throwing Rock. Tells are one reason why players study one another. Serious RPS players will spend time hunting for their tells and learning to suppress them.

This can be an on-going project, because suppressing one tell can sometimes create another.

Broadcasting False Tells

Of course, if you can suppress tells, you can also create them. This requires intense coordination and concentration, not to mention planning. In order to make advantageous use of a false tell, you must display the tell long enough for an opponent to notice its significance, then break the pattern at a crucial moment to score a win. Timing is everything. It won't help you to lose several points because of a false tell only to gain one when you break it.

Selecting a Throw

Once the prime has started, you have to make a choice. Will it be Rock, Paper, or Scissors? This is the most discussed and debated aspect of RPS, and the foundation of your strategy. How do you decide?

Chaos Play

Proponents of the "Chaos School" of RPS try to select a throw randomly. An opponent cannot know what you do not know yourself. In theory, the only way to defeat a random throw is with another random throw – and then only thirty-three percent of the time. Critics of this strategy insist that there is no such thing as a random throw. Human beings will always use some impulse or inclination to choose a throw, and will therefore settle into unconscious but nonetheless predicable patterns. The Chaos School has been dwindling in recent years as tournament statistics show the greater effectiveness of other strategies.

Gambit Play

The use of Gambits in competitive RPS has been one of the greatest and most enduring breakthroughs in RPS strategy. A "Gambit" is a series of three throws used with strategic intent. "Strategic intent" in this case, means that the three throws are selected beforehand as part of a planned sequence. Selecting throws in advance helps prevent unconscious patterns from forming and can sometimes reduce tells. Choosing throws in groups of three will prevent you from switching to a purely reactive game while leaving you numerous decision-points to keep the strategy adaptable.

The "Great Eight" Gambits

The mathematically inclined will quickly realize that there are only twenty-seven possible Gambits. All of them have been used and documented in tournament play. Each has several names from a variety of localities. There is no such thing as a "new" Gambit.

The "Great Eight" Gambits are the eight most widely used. There is nothing about these eight that make them superior to any other Gambits, although as a group they can be very effective. Several high-level players built careers on just these eight Gambits. They are, sorted alphabetically by their most common names:

Avalanche (RRR)

Bureaucrat (PPP)

Crescendo (PSR)

Dénouement (RSP)

Fistfull o' Dollars (RPP)

Paper Dolls (PSS)

Scissor Sandwich (PSP)

Toolbox (SSS)

Beyond Gambits

The strongest criticism of Gambit play is that players still have tendencies to develop patterns. Rather than throwing Rock when angry, a Gambit player may throw Avalanche, resulting in three lost points rather than just one. The true genius of Gambit play, however, is that Gambits can be used as building blocks of larger strategies.

Chain Gambits

"Chain Gambits" are one way of expanding Gambit strategies. A Chain Gambit is a series of five throws, or two Gambits joined by a common throw. For instance, "PSPSS" is a Chain Gambit built from Scissor Sandwich and Paper Dolls. By shifting one Gambit by one throw, a Chain Gambit can prevent your opponent from obtaining multiple successive victories even if she predicts which Gambit you're using next.

Combination Moves

Gambits and Chain Gambits can also be combined to form longer, complex Combination Moves. By planning your strategy in blocks of six or more throws, you can nearly eliminate reactive tendencies. The downside of Combination Moves is that they can tax the memory. Few things are as disconcerting as forgetting your strategy half way through it.

Exclusion Strategies

"Exclusive Strategies" have been getting a lot of attention lately. An Exclusive player will at least severely limit, if not neglect altogether, the use of one of the three throws. Hence, a "Rock Exclusive" player only throws Paper and Scissors. On the surface, such a strategy seems to give an opponent a serious advantage. By neglecting Rock, a player is vulnerable to Scissors.

Many opponents, however, will focus their entire strategy on predicting when the missing throw will appear – even if it never appears at all! A few players have experimented with "Double-Exclusive Strategies," using only one throw for a whole game, but the statistics gathered so far do not indicate this is as effective as Single-Exclusion.

Meta-Strategies

"Meta-strategies" go beyond selecting your throw. In fact, in many cases, their purpose is to let you select your opponent's throw! Meta-strategies are as numerous as shells on the beach, but they are all based on one of two principles.

The first is: "If you can make your opponent believe what you want him to, you can make him behave how you want him to." This is usually accomplished through pre-game conversation or in-game banter. No one ever said RPS was played in silence!

Getting Under Your Opponent's Skin

The second principle of meta-strategies is: "If you can make your opponent react to you, you can play the game for her." Many players will slip into reflexive habits and strategies when angry, frustrated, afraid, or confused. If you can get your opponent into that condition, you have the control of the match.

Classic Meta-Strategies

If your opponent figures out what you're up to, meta-strategies can backfire horribly. Worse than if you'd never used them, they can leave you confused and give your opponent control of the match. A good trainer can help you create and hone new meta-strategies as well as show you when to use them and when to leave well enough alone.

Here are a few well-documented meta-strategies to use as examples or as a starting point for building your own:

Old Hat

This is one of the oldest and most well-known meta-strategies of all time. Its effectiveness is minimized by the fact that nearly every player nowadays will recognize the "Ol' 'Old Hat'" but as it is the foundation of many more developed meta-strategies, this guide would be incomplete without it.

The purpose of the "Old Hat" strategy is to demoralize an opponent into feeling inferior or intimidated. Common "Old Hat" banter may include:

"I knew that would be your next move."

"This time, actually think before you throw."

"Rock? Hmmm. . . . Frankly I am surprised that Paper obviously didn't occur to you."

"I don't suggest using the Avalanche gambit on me; I did invent it, after all."

If you can successfully frustrate, anger, or make your opponent feel inferior, you may be able to drive him into a reactive game and take control of the match.

Crystal Ball

One of the more clever meta-strategies, "Crystal Ball" is a ploy to confuse an opponent and derail what might be an otherwise effective strategy. Like "Old Hat," this is a simple and time-tested strategy that is more effective as a foundation on which to build than used in its virgin form.

To employ "Crystal Ball," tell your opponent what she is going to throw:

"You're going to bring Scissors again, aren't you?"

If your opponent is unfamiliar with this ploy, you can now be certain she will not throw Scissors. That makes Paper a safe throw.

Rusty

"Rusty" is a dubious meta-strategy at best. A player using this technique will claim to be "out of practice" and predict his own defeat. This may put an opponent off her guard or instill a false sense of confidence, but this rarely has a significant effect on a match. Still, some players swear by it and continue to include it in their repertoire.

Probing Your Opponent

It is important to know what kind of player you are facing, their strength regarding how well they can match your abilities. Is it long-form game, a lightning round (one throw), best-of-three? In short matches, your best bet is to pick a good strategy or gambit and stick to it. In longer matches, you have the opportunity to "probe" your opponent.

Many players will develop and practice several distinct strategies. Often, after the first five or six throws, you can identify which strategy he is using. That helps you determine which of your strategies will be most helpful.

Consequently, many players develop a few opening sequences, from three throws to ten, that are independent of their larger strategies. The only purpose of these openings is to get a sense of how an opponent is going to play the match

The Backup Plan

Okay, so it's not working. She's got your strategy licked and you're dropping farther and farther behind. Don't panic! You've got a backup plan, right?

When you're down, the thing to avoid is slipping into reflexive or reactive patterns. You'll become predictable, your opponent will take control of the match, and you will lose your chance to recover the win.

A better approach is to develop and practice several independent strategies. Some techniques will work wonders against one opponent and fail miserably against the next.

It's not always easy to know when to switch tactics. Even if you lose three or four throws in a row, your opponent may still be in the dark about what you're doing. With experience and practice, though, you'll learn to tell if your opponent has you figured out.

Keeping it Varied

Finally, never stop working on your strategy! Your opponents are studying you as carefully as you're watching them. Any strategy, no matter how complicated, can be unraveled if you repeat it often enough. Change. Adapt. Replace old tactics with new approaches. Keep your game fresh, and you'll keep your opponents guessing!

GAMBITS OF ROCK PAPER SCISSORS

The Rock Paper Scissors game is an exciting game. It requires a lot of skillfulness, mindfulness, and preparations. Between playing the game for fun and winning the opponent lies the necessity to create a powerful winning strategy. In building strategies for an RPS match, the player needs to understand the crucial existence of gambit. In The Master's Guide to Rock Paper Scissors, a gambit is (a series of three successive moves made with strategic intent." Thus, the artful use of gambits in RPS matches will show how much the player has mastered the game.

There are popular eight gambits known as the Eight Great Gambits. These gambits are considered to be the most widely acclaimed, mostly used, and historically significant set of gambits as far as the Rock Paper Scissors game is concerned. As you will see in this article, these gambits have a specific intent. It is therefore understood that an RPS player must organize his plays into gambits in order to be able to dominate the game and avoid losing focus. Players with planned strategies are more likely to win matches compared to those who did not set up playing patterns.

Let us look at the Eight Great Gambits:

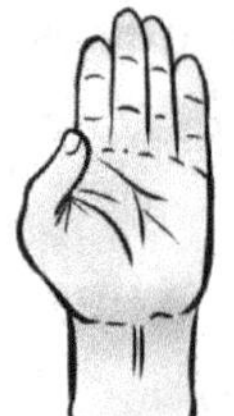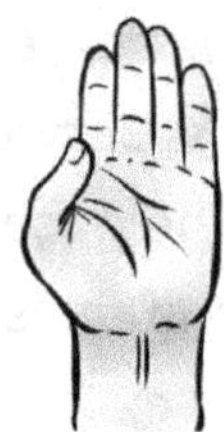

**The Bureaucrat
(Paper Paper Paper)**

The bureaucrat is formerly referred to as Confetti. This gambit is represented by throwing Paper in three successive throws (Paper Paper Paper). The Rock Paper Scissors System understands the bureaucrat to be used as the ultimate strategy in passive-aggressive play. Usually, the first throw for beginners is the Rock, making it a little difficult for the opponent to survive the first round. As a result, it is relatively easy for the opponent to decide to throw Paper in the expectation that the opponent will throw a Rock. A player that dwells too much or makes the mistake of throwing Rock will not last in the game. It will be an easy run if the player fails to change his hands.

**Avalanche
(Rock Rock Rock)**

The avalanche is a combination of Rocks in three successive throws usually intended to make an aggressive impact. Although it should be noted that the avalanche is a little subtle, still, the combo has an offensive intention. This gambit combo is developed in the late 1800s. Usually, the Rock is recognized as a throw accompanied by bravado, recklessness, courage, overconfidence, and arrogance. The Rock is also used as a protective maneuver. Since it is the commonest of all throws, players are quick to change hands to Rock, especially in matches where the thrower is being dealt with by his opponent.

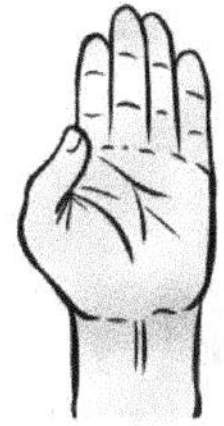  

The Crescendo
(Paper Scissors Rock)

As the name implies, the Crescendo is a combo of three throws that slowly builds a devastating effect on the opponent. The combo is played by first throwing Paper then followed by Scissors and Rock. The series gives the play an elegant picture, thus creating an increasing effect. The shattering impact of Rock is what categorizes the height of the effect.

  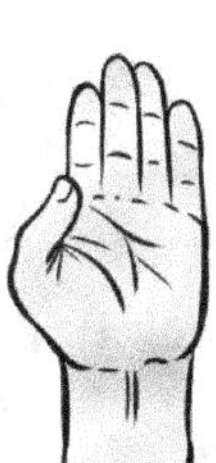

Denouement
(Rock Scissors Paper)

This combo is represented by the first throw of Rock to make an aggressive entry, followed by subtle submission of Scissors and Paper. It describes a cooling-down approach, also forcing the opponent into a difficult situation. The gambit is the direct opposite of the Crescendo. While the Crescendo offers and increasing effect, Denouement is rather cooling down the effect.

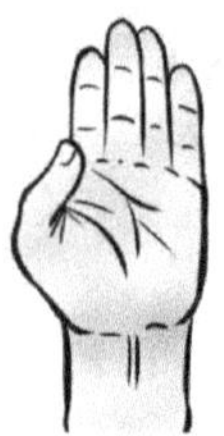

**Paper Dolls
(Paper Scissors Scissors)**

Paper suffocates Rock. Scissors cuts Paper. Although this series is complex in the process of making, it comes with simple interpretation. The initial throw of Paper handles Rock, leveling the playing field but then tracks back to protect the player. This gambit is quite effective against a player that is unaware. The strategy is often used to push for an early offense. For instance, if Paper suffocates Rock or loses to Scissors, the subsequent throws of quick and sneaky Scissors will either sustain the win or balance the game. A player that is careless and not sharp enough to read the game will fall quickly in the hands of this gambit.

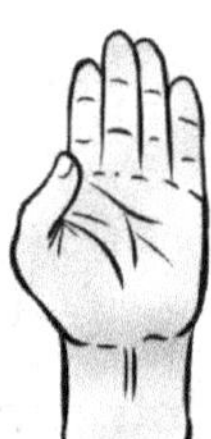

**Fistful O'Dollars
(Rock Paper Paper)**

This gambit is interpreted by throwing Rock at first and changing to Paper for the two following throws. It is categorized by aggression and then followed by the balance of power. The rapid switch from being offensive to being defensive is a tricky play that can put the opponent in a very difficult position. As much as this gambit can win the game for the thrower, it may also cost him the match if the opponent takes the risk of sustaining Scissors in two successive throws. This gambit continues to be one of the best offensive moves since taking the 1976 RPS World Championship by great surprise.

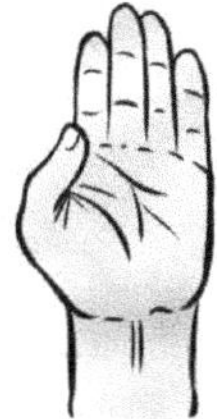  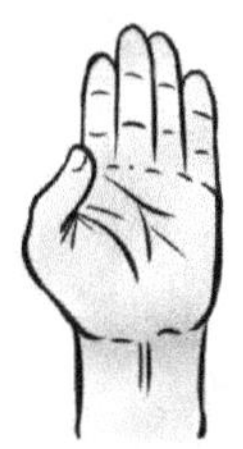

Scissor Sandwich
(Paper Scissors Paper)

This is another one of the offensive gambits. Although it is not the most offensive, however, it also creates a powerful effect by unsettling the opponent through the use of the concealed Scissors. This gambit is considered very evasive and devious as it keeps the opponent in the dark.

Toolbox
(Scissors Scissors Scissors)

The use of Scissors in a Rock Paper Scissors game comes with dexterity and intentionality. It can be said that the Scissors hand gesture is the most difficult of all the three hand gestures in the game. This is because of the force required in order to form the "V" shape while holding the ring finger and pinky with the thumb. Therefore, any player that intends to use this gambit in an RPS match must be sure of himself. The throw requires steady nerves and steady hands. The inability to properly and effectively display this hand gesture may attract penalties ranging from a warning to ejection from the match. One other danger that circles the use of toolbox is the risk that comes with using it against beginners.

Beginners are quick to choose the powerful crushing Rock. Therefore, it is not suggested that a player should opt for this gambit against beginners.

TELLS IN ROCK PAPER SCISSORS

Rock, Paper, Scissors is a mere hand game with several names and variations. And so you know, it is played around the world and is most times used the surest way of making decisions on issues. In some cases, RPS is even played for sport. The rules require that opposing players use one hand to form one of three shapes at an agreed-upon time. The person that plays the most resilient "object" is the winner of the game. Yup, it is that easy! Rock, Paper, Scissors is a game that just anybody can play and win. There is no fundamental advantage to the stronger, older, or more experienced player.

So, you are already aware of what is involved in playing the Rock Paper Scissors game; however, have you thought about ways you could easily win in this game? If you have a specific strategy that works for you, it will, in no time, turn you into an expert in the game.

Nonetheless, just like every other game with contestants and a need for a winner, RPS has its tells that would naturally help very observant players to win without much fuss.

In case you are in the dark about tells in a game, let's try to explain that as well. Tells are the unconscious gestures displayed by players during the game. It can come in several forms, for instance, eye movements, facial expressions, galvanic skin response, stance, muscle tension, and other forms of body movements.

Now, for you to comfortably understand the gesture displayed by your opponent during a tournament requires self-awareness and keen eyes that is perfected most of the time in front of a mirror. It is important to note that not everyone loves standing in front of the mirror and practicing tells. In fact, some players attribute such practices to foolishness. There is no doubt that it is absolutely true. Standing in front of the mirror, moving your face and other parts of your body, sure sounds strange. One can decide to overlook the mirror method and videotape oneself while doing it.

When a player becomes aware of tells and their importance, such a player can try as much as possible to minimize its use during any match and thus leaving such a player unpredictable and a potential winner. In trying to do away with any signs of tells, a player should take a comfortable stance before anything. The idea behind a comfortable posture is that when the body is relaxed, there is little or no muscle tension and, thus, fewer muscular tells. Sadly, the eye and facial tells are almost impossible to eliminate. In this article, however, we have taken the pain of listing the possible tells and how it can be eliminated to the barest minimum.

Different Tells in Rock, Paper, Scissors

The angle of the arm: professional players in RPS have the tendency of playing an upright Paper. This is because, if the Paper throw is gestured in some other way, one can quickly tell when such a player is trying to play the Rock and Scissor since they would turn their arms to play.

Rock Jaw: the rock jaw is the name given to the tells observed when there is tension in the opponent's jaw right before they play the Rock throw.

Cement Fist: when there is a noticeable tension around the knuckles, then there is a likelihood that the player is about to play the Rock gesture.

Placement of the thumb: if your rival has their thumb on top of the hand, then chances are, such an opponent is less likely to play Scissors because it is absolutely harder to throw by now. Nonetheless, professional players tend to keep their thumb by the side of the hand instead of on top.

Paper Hook: Some players have some level of affinity for curving their hand during the approach to the body right before they make the Paper gesture. When playing against an opponent, the paper hook looks like a backward 'C' when the opponent is right-handed.

In order to be able to play without exposing any tells, it is important to learn about the tells as earlier listed.

Now during these tournaments, players, most of the time, prepare their sequence of three gestures. This they do right before the game begins. Some tournament players develop strategies to confuse or convince the other player to make an illegal move, resulting in a loss. Well, these are some of the things you get to do if you really want to be really good at this game.

One of such strategies is to shout the name of one move right before throwing another. This is done solely to confuse and misdirect the opposing player. You can imagine the look on your opponent's face when he expects you to throw a Rock, and you come up with Paper. Or when you are playing with a professional player, they give a fake tell just to mislead you.

Broadcasting False Tells

This is also a type of tells. The essence of this tells is to effectively mislead your opponent during a game. What a player does with this is to intentionally display fake eye cues, stance, facial expressions, and fake muscular gestures simply to misdirect the opponent. Now, one thing about this move is, it is expected to be used on professional players. Using it on rookies would be a simple waste since they may not be aware of tells yet.

If you plan to make use of this tells, be sure not to put on hand gloves, sunglasses, or the effect may not be noticed.

Anyway, if you are really looking forward to winning RPS games, you should have some tips in the back of your mind.

Throw Paper against a male challenger. Statistics have shown that inexpert males lead with Rock most of the time for their first move in the RPS game. Now, by throwing Paper on your first move against them, you stand a greater chance of winning them.

Throw Rock against a female challenger. This is funny but true. Most women tend to lead with Scissors, so if you throw out a Rock on the first play of the game, you are sure to win such an opponent.

Observe to be sure your opponent is using the same move twice in a row. If your competitor plays the same action twice in a row, chances are, they are not likely to use it a third time. So, you can assume they are not going to throw that move anymore. Put out a gesture that will give you either a stalemate or win, ensuring you won't lose.

ROCK PAPER SCISSORS GAME THEORY

The Rock Paper Scissors game has a very rich history. The history which emphasizes the origin and creation of the game also contains the nature and ways to understand the game. It should be noted that the Rock Paper Scissors game possesses a complex organization. Nonetheless, the complexities that surround the game, the simple interpretations that abound in the game make it interesting as it offers it a simple outlook. Apart from the interpretations that offer simplicity to the game, one cannot but notice the exciting nature of the game. The game's nature creates a form of fun atmosphere but also promotes healthy competition between players.

The competition between the players is based on the necessity to establish who is better and who is not. As a result, there is a playing ground that offers both players the chance to dominate and exert their authority. Although the playing ground offers equal chances of survival, however, some other factors may give either of the players an upper hand in the game such as level of experience and years of experience in standard tournaments. As a result of the existence of these factors, every RPS player must train himself to the point that he masters the game and is able to exert his dominance.

This means the player must be ready to devote to learning the Rock Paper Scissors game and the complexities surrounding it. Doing this will help the player understand the rudiments of the game and increase his ability to form effective strategies that can win him RPS matches. The failure to come to terms with what the

RPS game demands will often cause the player to fall easily against a deserving opponent. One of the things that should be noted when it comes to the RPS game is that it has a psychological effect on the player. In the same way that winning boosts the player's morale and confidence in the game, losing also has a devastating effect. In other words, constant losing may break the player's passion for the game and eventually make him quit.

For someone who intends to last in the game and also embrace the chances of winning, he must first acquire some knowledge that is crucial to the mastery of the game. Practice alone is not enough to become a pro in the Rock Paper Scissors game. The truth even is that you need to know what to practice. One of the things you must learn about the RPS game is the theory that has been accepted to be applicable in the game. The theory explains the elements present in the game, their interpretations, and their applications. Like every other game, theories describe the essence of the game which every participant must understand and follow.

Why Are The Theories Involved

The theories in the Rock Paper Scissors game are formed to afford the game a peculiar and unique nature. These theories equally serve as the mode of play of the game, which allows players to showcase their dexterity, experience, and superiority. These theories are a must-know for every person that has an interest in the game. Also importantly, the theories offer the guidelines and code of play of the game. It is therefore correct to say that the theories in the Rock Paper Scissors game are an essential part of the elements that sum up what RPS game is and how it works. The firm grasp of the RPS game theories will go a long way in improving a player's professionalism.

Simple But Interesting Interpretations

The Rock Paper Scissors gameplay makes the game even more interesting to play. The introduction of moves designed to have distinct interpretations and effects and the general outlook of the game are what constitute the fascinating appearance of the game. Apart from the game offering a healthy competition between players, it also sustains a good mood as the game is designed to offer pleasure and enjoyment. One thing that should be noted is that the theories of the game are created based on the elements available for use in the game.

It is simple. The game requires both players participating in the game to make any of the three generally accepted throws (Rock Paper Scissors). These three elements possess different explanations that are crucial to the calculations in the game. Let us consider the representations of these moves as well as their calculations:

- The Rock is represented by a closed fist extended toward the opponent. To prevent bodily harm, it is prohibited for a player to hit the opponent with his closed fist. By calculation, Rock crushes Scissors but will lose to Paper. Where both players throw Rock at the same call, it is a tie, and there will be a rethrow.

- The Paper is represented by an open palm extended in the form of a handshake toward the opponent. The interpretation of this move is that Paper wins a throw of Rock but loses to Scissors. A rethrow is called if there is a tie.
- The Scissors is represented by making a "V" shape toward the opponent. The way this move is interpreted is that Scissors cuts Paper but is crushed by Rock.

The three moves have a trinity relationship in that one beats the other. Every player must be well-grounded in these moves in order to understand how to calculate their moves.

The Importance Of The Theories

The importance of the RPS game theories cannot be overemphasized. They are the spirits of the game, and we have discussed part of them in this article. The game elements and interpretations are crucial to the successful outcome of an RPS match.

THE STUDY AT ZHEJIANG UNIVERSITY ABOUT ROCK PAPER SCISSORS

The problem of how to win at Rock Paper Scissors has, believe it or not, overwhelmed mathematicians and game theorists for a very long time. While they formerly had invented a theoretical answer to the question, an experiment by Zhijian Wang at Zhejiang University in China that made use of real players has discovered an exciting crinkle to the original theory.

The recreation area game of Rock Paper Scissors may not appear like one in which players take a scientific approach. However, that is precisely what three Chinese scientists revealed. Since these disclosures, their findings were circulated in a research paper that won them a Best of 2014 by MIT Technology Review. The article was also published at the esteemed Massachusetts Institute of Technology in Cambridge.

Zhou Haijun is part of the Institute of Theoretical Physics of the Chinese Academy of Science. Wang Zhijian and Xu Bin of the Experimental Social Science Laboratory at Zhejiang University wrote a paper titled Social Cycling and Conditional Responses in the Rock Paper Scissors Game.

According to a statement released by Zhejiang University in Hangzhou, this was the first time Chinese scientists would win this prize in the social science realm. And the publication was worth it because it revealed a pattern of choices players make during the RPS game.

According to the article published by Zhijian, the Rock-Paper-Scissors (RPS) game is a commonly used model system in game theory. Evolutionary game theory forecasts the existence of obstinate cycles in the evolutionary paths of the game. The article further claimed that the experimental evidence has remained to be feeble.

In the experiment, Zhijian observed that winning players have a habit of sticking with their winning tactic. In contrast, losers have a tendency to switch to the next line of attack in the sequence of rock paper scissors, following what he calls "persistent cyclic flows."

Okay, enough of the terms; let' get into what the article was really all about. Here's how it works in the run-through: Player A and Player B both start using unplanned methods. If Player A goes ahead to use Rock and Player B throws Paper, Player A is defeated. In the succeeding round, Player A can take on the mindset that Player B will use Paper again and should, for that reason, use Scissors to beat the opponent. In the next round, because Player B was defeated, Player A can assume that Player B will use the subsequent strategy in the sequence - Scissors — and then Player A should then use Rock, thus winning again.

If you take the game on a theoretic level, the most statistically right way to play Rock Paper Scissors is by picking your approach at random. Now, since there are three possible outcomes - a loss, a win, or a tie - and each approach has at least one strategy that would easily defeat it and another strategy that the throw can defeat. Well, for the experiment, the strategy that a player wins with is not the concern. Nonetheless, it makes more sense to pick Rock exactly one-third of the time, Scissors one-third of the time, and Paper one-third of the time. And this is called the Rock Paper Scissors' Nash equilibrium.

Even with the Nash Equilibrium presenting the best strategy for a real-life Rock Paper Scissors game, Zhijian, in his study, found an absolutely different pattern when he and two other researchers enrolled about seventy-two students to play the game. The group of researchers divided the students into twelve groups of six players and had them each play about three rounds of Rock Paper Scissors against each other. Yup, I know precisely what you are thinking, but this experiment needed lots of practice to give a theory. Zhijian also added some expenses in ratio to the number of victories.

When Zhijian reviewed the outcomes, he discovered that students selected each strategy close to one-third of the time, and thus proposing the Nash Equilibrium theory. Nonetheless, when he looked closer, he noted a more irregular pattern.

In this pattern that Zhijian found, winners were repeating their strategy, and losers kept moving to the next strategy in the sequence. This discovery, the group of researchers called a 'conditional response' in game theory. The researchers have theorized that the reaction may be hard-wired into the brain, an inquiry they may have to study with further necessary experiments.

As of now, Zhijian recommends that exploiting the knowledge that most players use the conditional tactics that may result in winning so many games in the Rock Paper Scissors.

To win the RPS game, players need to pay attention to the action their opponent just engaged in or the throw they made. Then they can quickly estimate how their opponents will act in subsequent throws and make the hand gesture that would beat their opponent's move.

Assuming a player wins by playing Rock, he is very likely to play Rock again in the next round, and this, according to Zhijian, has to do with the way the brain works. But if he is defeated, he will most likely shift to Paper in the next round.

According to MIT Technology Review, this game theory is known as a conditional response and has never been revealed before in game experiments.

Nevertheless, if the game Rock Paper Scissors were played by arbitrary number generators or robots, then the chances of forecasts an order for a good win in the game would have been so little no one would bother studying it. This is because each robotic player would aimlessly throw out one of the three signs, and over long enough sample sizes, and then, the games would be equally split between wins for player A, wins for player B, and ties making it a non-exciting game to see.

Thankfully, Rock Paper Scissors is hardly ever played by robots. Most of the time, it is played by humans that work emotionally and sometimes irrationally. The study carried out at Zhejiang University was not only a fantastic work, but it is also a good development for humanity.

ROCK PAPER SCISSORS TOURNAMENT ETIQUETTE

Some customs permeate the Rock Paper Scissors game, especially for standard tournaments. Individual preparations at certain levels, as well as the codes of conduct, are all important considerations that a player should make before he is ready for the tournament. This article will explain the popular practices in Rock Paper Scissors, particularly before and during the tournament. We will also discuss the rules that guide the behaviors of players and spectators during the tournament.

Hitting Hands

One of the troubles that the World RPS authorities had faced in times past is ritualizing winning. This comes with intentionally mimicking the real-life interpretations of the moves. In other words, players go for actual interaction of moves to signify the RPS calculations. For instance, Rock crushes Scissors. Mimicking a real-life interaction of these two moves would involve the Rock thrower deliberately hitting the Scissors, thereby forming a physical interaction. Ritualizing winning was a common practice in tournaments.

Sadly, the result was devastating. The physical contact often came with aggression leading to a hand injury. One such occasion was during a hotly contested semifinal match. In the process of ritualizing the win of Rock crushing Scissors, the Scissors suffered a torn ligament on his index finger. Due to this, the WRPSA banned the conduct and formed the no-contact rule for tournaments.

Pretournament Training

Players need to get ready for tournaments. This way, they are physically prepared and mentally ready for the matches they will play during the tournament. Among many preparations to be made, the following are crucial to getting ready for standard RPS tournaments.

Nutrition

The combination of foods the player eats may contribute to his performance during the tournaments. It is often contested which foods players should consume before their matches. All players should be concerned about their nutrition. As a result, the WRPSA advises players to consume brain foods like fish and drink a lot of liquids, particularly water. Also, players should not eat more than routine demands to avoid any stomach outburst during the tournament. Changing diet may put a player at risk during the matches.

Forearm Stamina

A player will play tons of matches in an RPS tournament. Therefore, every player must build his forearm stamina before the tournament starts. This he can do through repetitive practice of hand throws. The player is also advised to practice with his non-dominant hand. It is important to have an alternative in case of injury.

Learning The Opponent's Moves

Like every other competitive game, learning about the opponent is an important task. In an RPS tournament, a player should take time to review his opponent's previous matches in order to find patterns or modes of play that the opponent uses. Learning the opponent's strategies will help greatly when the player is forming his strategies.

Practice

Of course, practice cannot be underestimated in the Rock Paper Scissors game. Practice improves the player a lot and gets him ready for his next match. However, practice should not be done in a way that wears the player out. Instead, as much as there should be practice, the player should ensure his muscles are well-rested before the match. Resting the mind is also essential.

Conduct And Behaviors

Specific rules guide the conduct and behaviors of both the players and spectators in an RPS tournament. It is expected that the spectators and the tournament players are aware of these rules and guidelines. Generally, ignorance of the law is not an excuse;

therefore, an excuse for lack of information will not be considered on account of flouting any of the rules. The essence of the rules and regulations is to ensure everyone involved in the game composes themselves professionally and for the tournament's smooth run. The Rock Paper Scissors tournament will in no way agree with bad conduct or any act or omission that can dent the image of the game or disrupt the tournament proceedings. In order to prevent any hassle in the process, the RPS authorities have set some guidelines for both players and spectators in a standard and regulated RPS tournament. Let us consider the rules that guide the conduct and contribution of both of them.

Players

Below are general guidelines that guide the players' conduct and behaviors in the Rock Paper Scissors game. These guidelines are very important and should be considered sacred by every player. Failure to follow this etiquette may attract penalties ranging from a warning to ejection from the tournament hall.

- All players must appear at their starting time and ideally several minutes before to perform a final equipment check.
- A player should never consult or accept unsolicited information from a spectator. If this information is offered, the player should ignore it.
- Players should not cause unnecessary delays. In extreme cases delaying tactics may result in a penalty.
- While lighthearted verbal jockeying and jousting are permitted between players during the match, hurling insults and epithets is considered bad form and may be penalized by the referee.

- Players should note that in the absence of a referee, both players become referees-in-common and, as such, are entitled to discuss the game status and rule clarifications. Any disputes arising between the co-referees shall be resolved via RPS.
- All players should be familiar with the Players' Responsibility Code.
- Upon conclusion of the game, it is considered good form to acknowledge an adversary's presence, although a handshake is considered superfluous.
- RPS is a game without ties, so whether one wins or loses, conducting oneself with good grace is absolutely necessary.

Spectators

For the viewers, there are certain ways in which they must conduct themselves to ensure that the Rock Paper Scissors tournament goes as planned and without any issue whatsoever that can disrupt the game's proceedings. The following are what the audience must do while witnessing an RPS tournament.

- Spectators must refrain from making audible comments on the proceedings.
- Spectators need to abstain from any unnecessary movement within the players' field of view, such as excessive hand waving.
- Spectators should never offer advice to competitors or draw attention to a player's bungled strategy.

Photographers, camera operators, journalists, and groupies must allow sufficient room for players to maneuver.

RPS: TO PRACTICE OR NOT TO PRACTICE

The Rock Paper Scissors game is fun to play. At the same time, playing it comes with some level of skillset, experience, and a powerful combination of strategies. In other words, the RPS game offers an atmosphere of pleasure and enjoyment but also adds professionalism to its nature. This simply means that any player who wants to enjoy the game must be able to show that he has a strong grasp of the game. Sadly, many people who want to go into playing the Rock Paper Scissors game do not bother to go into the details of what the game entails. Instead, they desire that the game should give them the pleasure of playing and make them have a good time, even without learning the essentials of the game.

As a result of their ignorance, most end up losing interest in the game, not because their interest was not strong enough but because their intention toward playing the game was a bit misplaced. Do not get this wrong, the Rock Paper Scissors game is an interesting game and can be played to have a good time and enjoyment, especially in a social gathering or among siblings. But the fun part of it will never be achieved if one does not take time to learn and know how the game is played. In other words, the RPS game can only be fun and exciting to play for a person that knows how to play. What fun is it when the player does not understand the moves or their calculations and cannot build a combination of moves to form his strategies?

Now that we have established the necessity to know the game before you get to enjoy what it offers, there another clause that follows the task of learning the game. It should be noted that learning the Rock Paper Scissors game is not a onetime thing. Instead, it is a process that every player or anyone interested should continue. This is so because the RPS game tends to measure the level of professionalism between players. Although there is the idea of luck, luck only helps the one who has prepared. Preparation is the real deal when it comes to the Rock Paper Scissors game.

Learning the game is not enough; preparation should come before every RPS match as it goes a long way in improving the professionalism of the player. In essence, we are going to talk about practice. Practice in the RPS game has come under huge observation in recent years. The idea has been subjected to considerations from different levels. The one question that all considerations bother on is whether one needs to practice or not. The RPS game has a complex nature but comes with simple interpretations. Nonetheless, learning does not guarantee that you would reach the peak of professionalism at once. If that is so, does practice guarantee that you would be a master at it?

Practice is a continuous performance of one particular task to master it. In other words, the practice eventually becomes a habit. One of the best advice you will ever hear is that one should sustain any good habit that one has cultivated. In the same vein, how does practice sound in the RPS game? Practising RPS entails going over the moves and their interpretations over and over again. It involves being actively involved in forming strategies that can win you the match as well as learning mindfulness and improving your ability to read your opponent's mind. Practicing in RPS has to do with playing with people for the purpose of learning and understanding the game better.

Without a doubt, doing all these will immensely contribute to your mastery of the game, increase your level of professionalism, and improve your concentration and mindfulness. Do you still think practice does not work?

Having established the importance of practice, the level of practice should be considered next. The truth is that people practice on different levels. Also, people possess varying levels of assimilation. This means that as much as people practice differently, the amount of what they learn through practice will also be different. Therefore, it boils down to the question of how much a person should practice. Well, there is no one answer to this. The first thing to note is that good practice will help you develop more on the game. However, it is left to you to determine when and how you want to practice. The only thing we are after is that you practice, either on an average day or before your RPS game.

Does Practice Make Perfection?

There is a popular saying that practice makes perfect. The simple meaning is that continuous training will eventually help you master the game and hit the peak of professionalism. If practice offers you improvement, how much more a continuous practice? The simple idea that comes with this realization is that the more you practice, the more you become perfect. Those who do not practice run the risk of losing their touch of the game and falling easily at the feet of their opponents. Practice will make you perfect at the game, but it must be done with a high level of seriousness, commitment, and expectation.

Skills, Experience, And The Mind

It is important to note that practice involves a series of activities that should be handled continuously in order to reach perfection at all levels. The training, in this case, has to do with your dexterity, physical exercise as well as building mindfulness. Your practice can only hit perfection when train your hands, learn the strategies, learn to read the game, and learn to take risks during games. Again, professionalism is an essential consideration in RPS games, and the only way you can reach perfection is through continuous practice. Remember that practice not only improves your skills and your mind. It generally increases your experience level.

MEMBERSHIP TO THE WORLD ROCK PAPER SCISSORS ASSOCIATION

After reading this book you are now qualified to be a member in the World Rock Paper Scissors Association. In order to become a member, simply sign up:

www.wrpsa.com/membership

www.wrpsa.com

www.ingramcontent.com/pod-product-compliance
Lightning Source LLC
Chambersburg PA
CBHW061459250726
48657CB00005B/1667